Behavior Skills Printables Workbook:
for Students with Autism
&
Similar Special Needs

What's Included...	Page
Self-Monitoring	5
Self Control	7
Self-Control Cards	9
In Control or Out of Control?	11
Self-Control 2	13
Self Monitoring	15
Self-Monitoring Checklist 1	17
Self-Monitoring Checklist 2	19
Emotional Control	21
Staying Seated in Class	23
Is This Good Behavior?	25
Behavior Choices (Field of 2)	27
Breathe In, Breathe Out	29
Count to Ten	31
These are Things That Help Me...	32
These are Things That Calm Me...	33
How I Feel	35
What Should She do?	37
Classroom Rules	39
Organize This Desk	41
Transitions	43
What Order is This?	45
A Change in the Schedule	47
Making A Schedule	49
Cards to Help with Change	51
Making a Reading Schedule	53
Make Your Own Reading Schedule	55
Ways to Ask for the Bathroom	57
Bathroom Routine	59
Groups	61
What's the Deal with Transition?	63
During Math Tina Does This	65
Mini Schedule Template	67
Transition Phrases	69
Group Directions	71
Group Directions vs. Individual Directions	73
Waiting Area	75
Standing in Line	76
Who is Lining Up Correctly?	77
Hallway Behaviors	78
Transition Objects	79
Can you Carry That?	80

Behavior Skills Printables
BY: Autism Classroom

autismCLASSROOM.com

Self-Monitoring

This page is intentionally blank due to an activity on the next page.

Self Control

It is important to pay attention to your own behavior.

What is Self- Control?

Taking responsibility for my own behavior.

Thinking about what other people do.

This page is intentionally blank due to an activity on the next page.

Name:_____

Self-Control Cards

Point to each card. Make a thumbs up if they are showing self-control. Make a thumbs down if they are out of control. Match the correct word with the picture.

self-control | out of control | out of control | self-control

out of control | self-control | self-control | out of control

This page is intentionally blank due to an activity on the next page.

Name:_____

In Control or Out of Control?

Directions: Mark which sentence tells about this picture the best. Color the pictures that show "in control."

A	In control.
B	Out of control.

A	In control.
B	Out of control.

A	In control.
B	Out of control.

A	In control.
B	Out of control.

This page is intentionally blank due to an activity on the next page.

Name:_____

Self-Control 2

Behavior and self-control can be difficult. Do these pictures show self-control? Glue them in the correct spot.

YES	NO

YES	NO

This page is intentionally blank due to an activity on the next page.

15

Self Monitoring

Practice tracing the checkmarks.

Write a checkmark next to each skill.

To show good self-monitoring skills, I will...

 Keep my hands to myself.

Keep my feet to myself.

Stay in my seat during lessons.

 Use an inside voice.

This page is intentionally blank due to an activity on the next page.

Self-Monitoring Checklist 1

Create your own self-monitoring checklist. Cut and paste <u>3</u> skills you want to monitor.

☐	
☐	
☐	
☐	
☐	

Stay seated.

Do work.

Keep a quiet voice.

Listen to instructions.

Use my words.

Raise my hand if I have a question.

This page is intentionally blank due to an activity on the next page.

Self-Monitoring Checklist 2

Create your own self-monitoring checklist. Cut and paste 4 skills you want to monitor.

Hands to self.

Follow directions.

Quiet voice.

Inside voice.

Stay in my seat.

Keep my feet on the ground.

Do my work.

Use my words.

Look forward.

Work quietly.

Keep my pencil still.

Keep my hands in my work station.

Focus on my work.

Answer questions.

Participate in class.

Slow down and complete my work.

This page is intentionally blank due to an activity on the next page.

Behavior Skills Printables

Name:_____

Emotional Control

Directions: Match the picture to the correct word. Give a number to each volume level.

Upset

Frustrated

Nervous

Calm

3   2   4   1

This page is intentionally blank due to an activity on the next page.

Name:_____

Staying Seated in Class

Directions: Cut on the dashed lines. Match the yes and no to the correct way to show how to stay seated in class.

Stay seated in the same area with the other students.	Get up and walk around the room.

Yes | No

This page is intentionally blank due to an activity on the next page.

Name:_____

Is this Good Behavior?

Directions: Cut out the pictures. Next, fill out the chart.

No	Yes. Good Behavior.
No	Yes. Good Behavior.
No	Yes. Good Behavior.
No	Yes. Good Behavior.

This page is intentionally blank due to an activity on the next page.

Name:_____

Behavior Choices
(Field of 2)

Follow the directions to color or mark the behavior that the student should do.

Pick one.

Choose one.

Which one?

Make a choice.

Which should he do?

Pick.

Your choice.

Choose.

This page is intentionally blank due to an activity on the next page.

Breathe In, Breathe Out

Directions: Help the kids relax by ordering the steps in the relaxation sequence.

1

2

3

4

Breathe in, breathe out.

1 2 3 4 5 6 7 8 9 10

Directions: Cut then paste in order at the top of the page.

Close your eyes. ①

Breathe out. ③

Repeat 5 times. ④

Breathe in. ②

This page is intentionally blank due to an activity on the next page.

Name:_____

Count to Ten

Directions: If a person is upset they might try to count to ten to calm down. Sometimes when they think of counting, it takes their mind off of the thing that made them upset.

Count and color the dots from the upset boy to the calm boy.

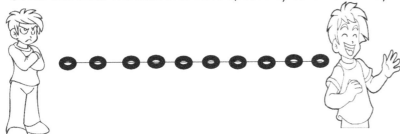

Count and color the dots from the upset boy to the calm boy.

Directions: Practice counting to ten using the large numbers below. Color in each number.

These are Things That Help Me...

Color or mark the things you like to use to help you stay organized.

Headphones

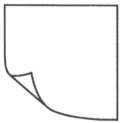

Sticky notes

A schedule

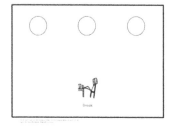

A token board

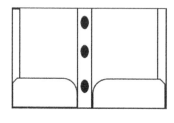

Folders

Physical boundaries

A walk break

First, Then board

Jumping

Chewing gum

Classroom signs

Name:_____

These are Things That Calm Me...

Directions: Mark the items that calm you.

Keep Calm

string

Sensory ball

exercise

Chewing gum

walking

pushing

squeezing

beanbag chair

headphones

The picture is not here.

Pictures shown: chewing gum-string-sensory ball-exercise-walking-pushing a wall-squeezing-beanbag-headphones-no picture here

This page is intentionally blank due to an activity on the next page.

HOW I FEEL

Directions: Cut and paste one sentence that describes how each person is feeling.

I feel scared.

My arm hurts.

I want to sleep.

Yes. I am having fun.

Today is a hot day.

This is frustrating.

My feelings are hurt.

This is great.

This page is intentionally blank due to an activity on the next page.

Name:_____

What Should She Do?

Tina is a student at school. She sits next to Justin at school. Today Tina hit Justin.

Directions: Paste 3 reasons why Tina might do that.

What should she do instead?

| The classroom is too loud. | Her ears hurt. | Her skin hurts. | She wants something. |

| She wanted to say hello. | She is angry. | She wants him to talk to her. | She does not want to do her work. |

| Keep her hands to herself. | Tell him what she wants. | Use her voice or her pictures cards. | Let the teacher know what is bothering her. |

This page is intentionally blank due to an activity on the next page.

Classroom Rules
What are some classroom rules?

Watch your veggies	Hands to self.	Listen.	Inside voice.
Tap the table.	Do your work.	Play all day.	Yell.

This page is intentionally blank due to an activity on the next page.

Organize This Desk

Cut out the pictures at the bottom of this page and paste them in the correct space to organize this desk.

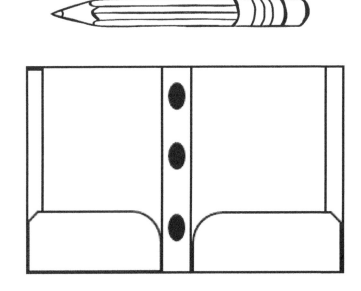

This page is intentionally blank due to an activity on the next page.

Transitions

This page is intentionally blank due to an activity on the next page.

Name:_____

What Order is This?

Directions: Cut out the definitions and glue them into the correct box.

Schedule.   **Match the name.**   **Match the order.**

lunch	1st
reading	2nd
opening	lunchtime
bus time	Right after lunch.
math	End of the day.

This page is intentionally blank due to an activity on the next page.

Name:_____

A Change in the Schedule

Dara was having a good day at school. She knew she would have gym class after lunch. Then, Ms. Green told her that reading was after lunch. Gym was cancelled and it was not after lunch. Dara loves gym. What should she do?

Cry and yell.

Fall on the floor.

Follow the new schedule.

Move the schedule card back to gym.

Hit someone.

Say No.

Tell herself that it will be ok.

Go to reading.

This page is intentionally blank due to an activity on the next page.

Making A Schedule

Making a schedule can help in many ways. It can tell you where to go. It can tell you what to do. It can tell you when you will be finished. It can help you know what is expected.

_____

_____

_____

_____

Directions: Put the sentences in order to copy the paragraph above about making a schedule.

It can tell you when you will be finished.

It can help you know what is expected.

Making a schedule can help in many ways.

It can tell you where to go.

It can tell you what to do.

This page is intentionally blank due to an activity on the next page.

Cards to Help with Change
Cut out the picture and match the picture to the card.

Teacher is Absent

Most days my teacher is at school. Sometimes my teacher is absent. It is ok when my teacher is absent. My teacher will be back another day. I can listen to the substitute teacher for that day.

A Change in the Schedule

Changes in my schedule can be hard. I like to know what is next. If there is a change, I can stay calm and do the different activity that my teacher tells me to do. It may be difficult, but I can give it a try.

A Favorite Activity is Cancelled

There are some activities I love to do. When they are cancelled I get upset. I will try not to get upset. I will remember that I will get to do the activity again at a later time.

This page is intentionally blank due to an activity on the next page.

Name:_____

Making a Reading Schedule

Raina needs a schedule to help her know what will happen during her lessons.
Help her by tracing the words and matching the pictures.

In Reading class, we will...

Read a book.

Match words.

Do a worksheet.

Finished.

This page is intentionally blank due to an activity on the next page.

Name:_____

Make Your Own Reading Schedule

Use the pictures to create your own reading schedule.

In Reading class, we will...

color   cut

read   worksheet

finished   write

match   identify

trace   sort

This page is intentionally blank due to an activity on the next page.

Name:_____

Ways to Ask for the Bathroom

Directions: Cut and paste the pictures in the correct box.

How should he tell "I need to use the bathroom."	What should he avoid doing?

say it   sign bathroom   use a picture   raise hand   running   staying quiet

This page is intentionally blank due to an activity on the next page.

Bathroom Routine

Directions: Cut on the dashed lines. Match the picture to the correct statement.

I will try to tell the adult when I need to use the bathroom.

I will try to walk quietly to the bathroom and use the bathroom.

I will wash and dry my hands.

I will go back to doing my work.

This page is intentionally blank due to an activity on the next page.

Name:_____

YES NO

Groups

Directions: Glue the correct answer in the box.

Leave the table.	
Leave the classroom.	
Stay with the group.	
Leave the school.	
Stay with the teacher.	

What do we do with our group?

YES | YES | NO | NO | NO

This page is intentionally blank due to an activity on the next page.

Name:_____

What's the Deal with Transition?

1

2

3

4

Why is it hard to make a transition?

Tommy is thinking of some reasons that making a transition is difficult. Match the numbers of each statement to see his reasons.

Next, color the number of the statement you agree with the most.

Directions: Cut then paste in order at the top of the page.

I don't want to leave what I am doing. ①

I don't want to go to the next activity. ③

I am scared of not knowing what to do. ④

It is too loud there. ②

This page is intentionally blank due to an activity on the next page.

Name:_____

During Math Tina Does This

It helps Tina to know what to expect in math class. Tell the order of Tina's schedule when taking math class.

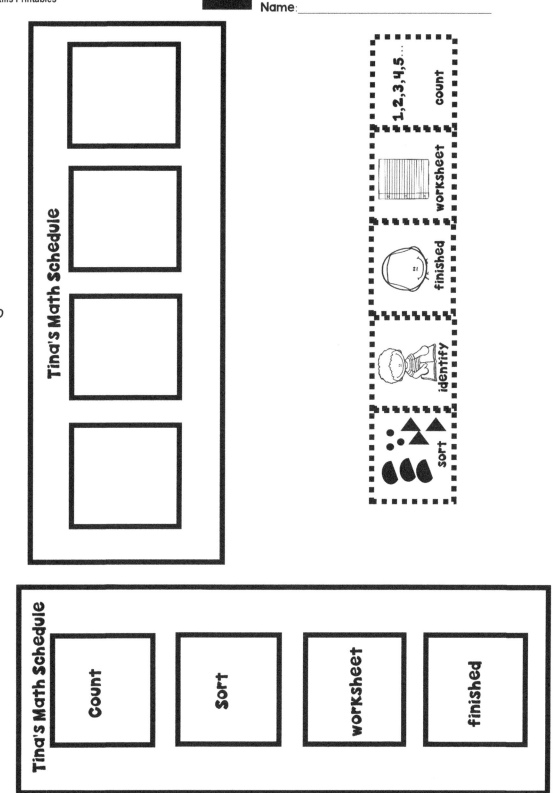

Tina's Math Schedule

count 1,2,3,4,5...

worksheet

finished

identify

sort

Tina's Math Schedule

Count

Sort

worksheet

finished

This page is intentionally blank due to an activity on the next page.

Name:_____

Mini Schedule Template

Practice scissor skills. Cut out this template and use this to create your own mini-schedule.

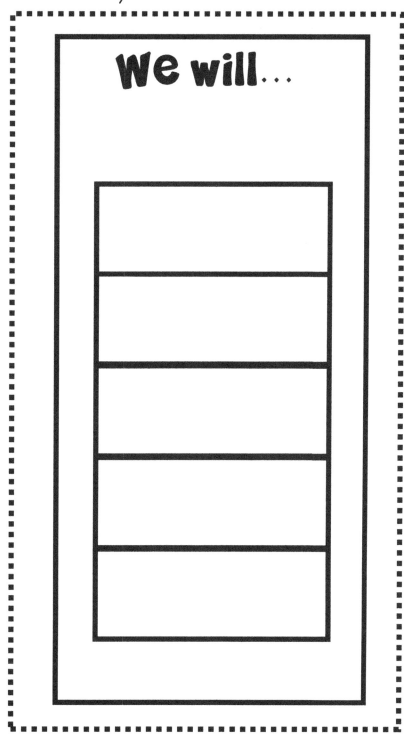

We will...

This page is intentionally blank due to an activity on the next page.

Transition Phrases

Mark the word **transition**.

transition	move	transition
share	transition	trade

Transition Phrases

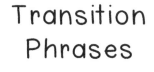

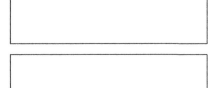

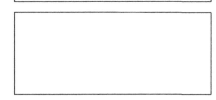

Cut and paste in the right column.

Time for our next activity.

Go to the next area.

Let's switch.

Clean up.

This page is intentionally blank due to an activity on the next page.

Group Directions

Directions: Read each circle. Mark all of the directions that a teacher could use when they are talking to you.

Let's go.

Come on.

Time to go.

Kids, line up.

Friends, keep walking.

Everyone, stand up.

Marsha, come here.

I need to see Leo.

Remember, the teacher does not have to call your name to be talking to you.

This page is intentionally blank due to an activity on the next page.

Group Directions vs. Individual Directions
Directions: Cut and paste any 2 sentences that describe each picture.

Let's go.	You go to centers.
Come on.	Everyone go to lunch.
Everybody line up.	Jimmy is going to his lesson.
Friends, time for us to go to the reading area.	Time for you to go to speech.

This page is intentionally blank due to an activity on the next page.

Waiting Area

waiting area

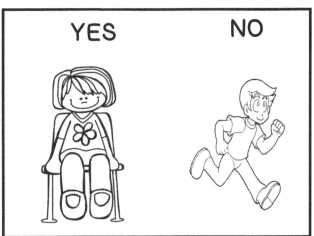

YES   NO

Wait:
To stay where you are and sit or
stand still.
Directions: Circle the correct word that matches
the definition.

listen	wait	leave

WRITE IT !!!

wait

_ _

Color the clothes of the girl who is waiting in the middle.

Mark the word **wait.**	Mark the words **sit down.**	Mark the word **stand.**
wait wait jump	sit down swim jog	stand stand gallop
leave wait zip	run sit down sit down	stand go waltz

Standing in Line

Directions: Start at the beginning of the line and draw to the end of the line.

Beginning .... End

Front ------------------------------- Back

Beginning ------------------------------- End

Front ------------------------------- Back

Beginning   End

Front   Back

Mark the word line.			
line	line	said	stand
line	climb	foot	line

Name:_____

Who is Lining Up Correctly?

Directions: Color in the circle of the kids lining up correctly.

Name:_____

Hallway Behaviors
Directions: Trace over these words.

quiet voices

watch teacher

line up

wait

listen

Name:_____

Transition Objects

Draw a line from the name of the transition object to the picture.

toy car

schedule card

ball

bin

beads

sensory toy

bathroom

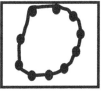

Can you Carry That?

Sometimes it helps to carry something from one area to the next to avoid leaving the group, darting, or showing inappropriate behaviors.

<u>Directions:</u> Circle 4 items that can be carried from one area to the next area.

schedule card

basket

lunch bin

A slide

large sign

first then board

Work Behaviors

This page is intentionally blank due to an activity on the next page.

Name:_____

Finish the Pattern (Work First, Then Play)

Directions: Finish the pattern.

Work	Play	Work	Play	Work	

Directions: Finish the pattern.

		Work		Work	

Directions: Finish the pattern.

Play

This page is intentionally blank due to an activity on the next page.

Name: ________________________

I am Working For It !

Draw a line to match the word on the top to the image on the bottom.

toy	ball	trampoline	computer	tablet	walk

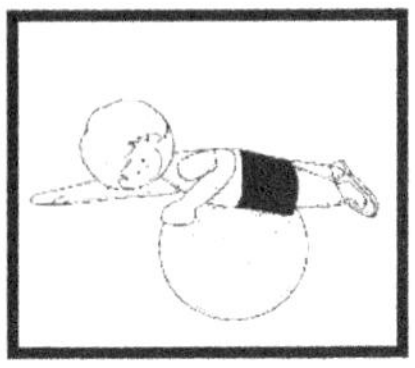

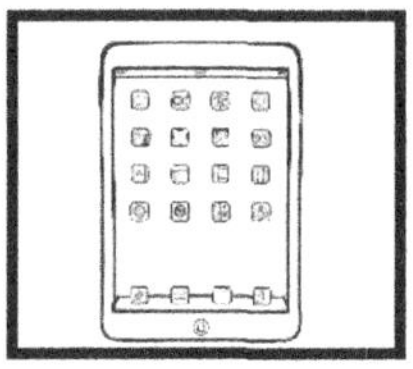

What is your favorite thing to work for?

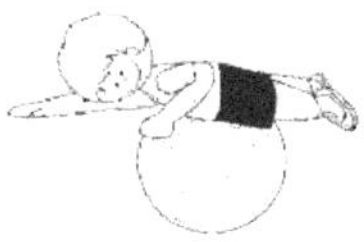
ball

trampoline

toy

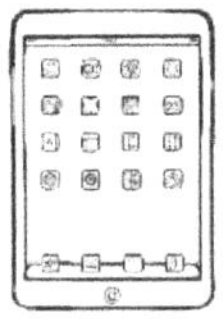
tablet

computer

walk

The picture is not here.

This page is intentionally blank due to an activity on the next page.

Name:_____

Make Your Own Incentive Chart

Directions: Cut out the chart and the pictures. Laminate or use contact paper to cover the chart. Place the item you want to work for in the bottom square. Try to earn 3 tokens (circles) to get the item.

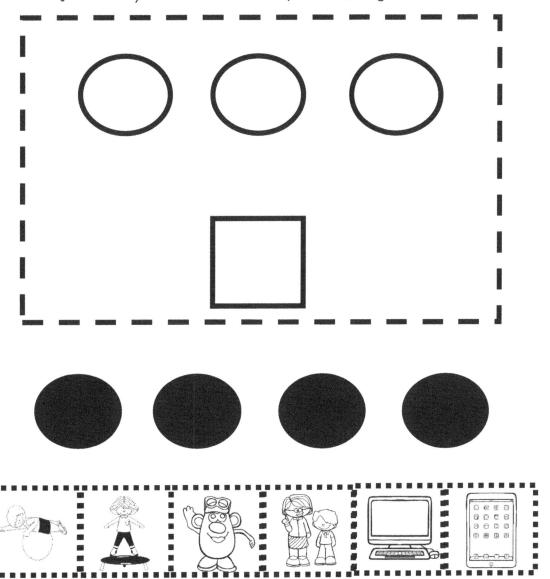

This page is intentionally blank due to an activity on the next page.

Name:_____

Expected Behaviors for Work Time

Directions: Draw a line from the expected behavior to the picture.

Raise your hand if you need help.	**Stay seated.**	**Work quietly.**

Directions: Check the 2 boxes that tell more expected behaviors for work time.

☐ Listen to directions.

☐ Go to the store.

☐ Finish your work.

This page is intentionally blank due to an activity on the next page.

Alternatives to Hitting

Name:_____

Directions: Cut on the dashed lines. Put in the 4 things you should try instead of hitting.

Try this.

use words   sign for help   use a picture   raise hand   hit   push

This page is intentionally blank due to an activity on the next page.

Name:_____

Behaviors for Work Time

Directions: Cut and paste the pictures in the correct box.

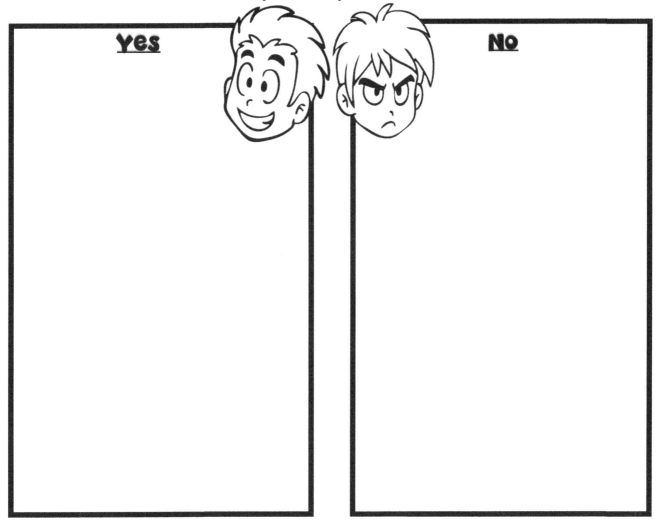

Yes   **NO**

grab   sit   hit   kick   do the task   leave

This page is intentionally blank due to an activity on the next page.

Name:_____

Interfering Behaviors

This student is showing the wrong behavior. Help the student correct the behavior. What are some good options the student can use instead?

Should this student kick another person?

yes	no

Should you kick another person?

yes	no

Keep Calm

What can the student do instead of kicking?

use words   get frustrated   hit someone   calm & count to ten   raise hand

kick   squeeze   take a walk   use a picture card

Color in the word.

Headphones

When is a good time to use headphones?

○ Yes
○ No

○ Yes
○ No

○ Yes
○ No

When I'm frustrated.   When it's too loud.   In a crowd.

Mark 2 ways to tell that you want headphones.

○ Hit someone.

○ Say "I want headphones."

○ Point to a picture of headphones.

WRITE IT !!!

headphones

_____

- - - - - - - - - - - - - - - - -

_____

Fill in the circle that shows headphones.

○

○

○

Request a Break

<u>Directions</u>: Color the yes circle green and the no circle red. Cut out the pictures below. Glue them into the appropriate box to show how to request a break.

YES   "I need a break."   **NO**

Correct Way

Raise your hand.

Use a break card.

Tell the teacher with words.

Finish your work.

Incorrect

Fall out on the floor.

Cry.

Bite.

Hit.

Raise your hand.

Cry.

Hit.

Fall out on the floor.

Bite.

Break Card

Use a break card.

Tell the teacher with words.

Finish your work.

This page is intentionally blank due to an activity on the next page.

Off Task (Visual Cue)
Directions: Trace over these words.

daydreaming

sidetracked

off task

play

Do your work.

Superhero thinks doing my work is important

My focusing cue.

Directions:
Use your creativity do these tasks.

1. Color in the left visual cue to help with focusing.
2. Draw, print out, or cut from a magazine, your own visual cue in the right box to help you remember to do your work.
3. Cut out the cards and use them when you need a reminder.

My focusing cue.

This page is intentionally blank due to an activity on the next page.

Activity Schedule

Directions: Help Jim create his activity schedule by matching the numbers.

Jim's Schedule

1	2	3	4

Read story. 1

Play video game. 4

Do worksheet. 2

Color picture. 3

This page is intentionally blank due to an activity on the next page.

Name:_____

First, Next Schedule

Directions: Color in the picture using the directions at the bottom of the page.

FIRST	NEXT
reading	recess

LOOK FOR	DO
One teacher sitting in a chair.	Color her shirt blue.
Grass on the playground.	Color it green.
Many kids sitting in class.	Color their hair brown.
Two kids sitting on swings.	Color their shoes red.
One girl sliding down a slide.	Color pants blue.

Behavior Skills Printables

3 Steps to Following Directions

Imitate Motor Movements
listen

Teacher Directions: Ask the student to "listen" while you say an action word.

Imitate Motor Movements
watch

Teacher Directions: Ask the student to "watch" while you do that action word.

Directions: Circle the words listen, watch and do.

run   **watch**   **don't**

listen   **close**   **do**

Imitate Motor Movements
do

Teacher Directions: Ask the student to "Do this" while modeling the action word.

Directions: Listen, watch, then do. Color the boy's shirt black.

Name:_____

These are Things That I Would Work For...

Color or mark the things that you would work for.

Listen to music

A therapy ball

Trampoline break

Dough

Break

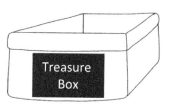

A treasure box

Shaving cream

A walk

Food

tickles

The picture is not here.

It's not here.

This page is intentionally blank due to an activity on the next page.

Name:_____

Task Analysis

Directions: Number the task analysis for checking the schedule. (Write in the numbers or use the numbers at the bottom of the page.)

Checking the Schedule

☐ Finish your activity.

☐ Remind yourself to check the schedule.

☐ Look at your schedule.

☐ Find the next activity on the schedule and walk to the next activity.

☐ Sit down at the next activity.

☐ Do your work.

This page is intentionally blank due to an activity on the next page.

Name:_____

Avoid Task Avoidance

Directions: Dot a circle that shows the proper way to respond when asked to do your work.

read
or
yawn

leave
or
sit down

work
or
hit

This page is intentionally blank due to an activity on the next page.

Being Around Others

Behavior Skills Printables

Name:_____

Stamp Out Un-Expected Behaviors

Directions: Dot or color each circle that shows an unexpected behavior that the students should avoid.

Name:_____

Non-Edible Objects

Directions: Not everything is made for us to eat. This student is confused about what to eat. What is appropriate for her to taste?

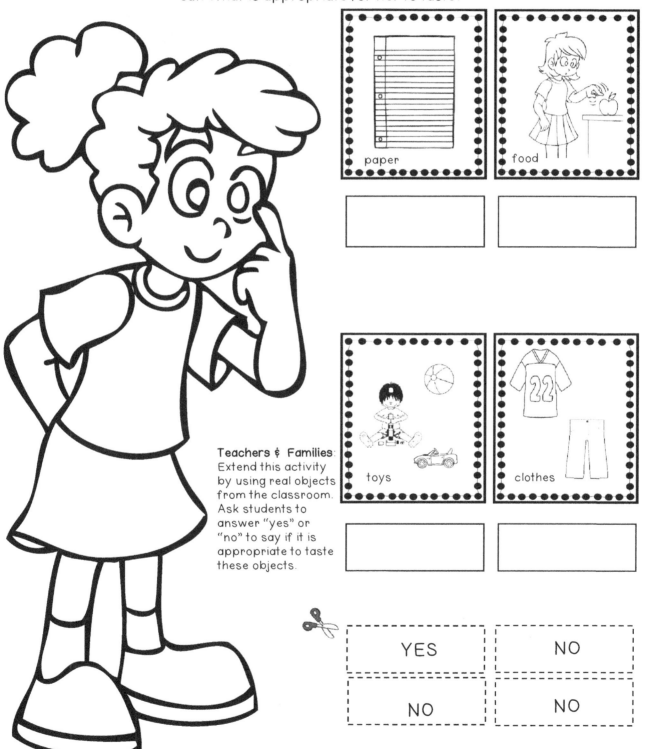

paper

food

Teachers & Families: Extend this activity by using real objects from the classroom. Ask students to answer "yes" or "no" to say if it is appropriate to taste these objects.

toys

clothes

YES	NO
NO	NO

This page is intentionally blank due to an activity on the next page.

Name:_____

Good Behavior
Color by Code
Directions: Color by the code.

LOOK FOR	DO
10 kids sitting and listening to the teacher.	Color their hair brown.
A boy smiling and waving hello.	Color his shirt yellow.
A boy cleaning up the toys.	Color his pants blue.
A friend sharing a pencil with another friend.	Color their hair black.

I Don't Want To Do This, What Do I Do?

What is a good way you should respond if you do not want to do something?

Behavior Skills Printables

Name:_____

Hands Off

These kids were playing at recess. One of them started to push the other boy. Pushing others is wrong. If you push someone, they could get hurt. It is a better idea to use your words or use a picture to tell what you want or to tell what you feel.

What should this boy do?

☐ Keep his hands to himself.

☐ Push someone.

Read the sign below. Color the outside square black. Color the square in the middle yellow.

KEEP YOUR
HANDS TO
YOURSELF

How might friends feel if you push them? Trace the words that relate to how they might feel if they are pushed.

cry
sad
hurt
scared

Name:_____

Aggressive Behaviors

What does it mean to "keep your hands to your self"?

☐ To grab or push someone.

☐ To stop your hands from touching, hitting or hurting someone.

Directions: Circle the student who is _not_ keeping hands to self.

Directions: Circle the student who _is_ keeping hands to self.

You Want To Get An Item: What Can You Do?

Directions: Trace over these words of behaviors you can do to get an item.

Ask.

Give a picture icon.

toy truck

Use a communication book.

MY Communication BOOK

Nodding Yes or No

If you do not have pictures and you cannot say "yes" or "no", you can still show that you mean yes or no. You can do this by nodding your head "yes" or shaking your head "no". Practice using the guided arrows below.

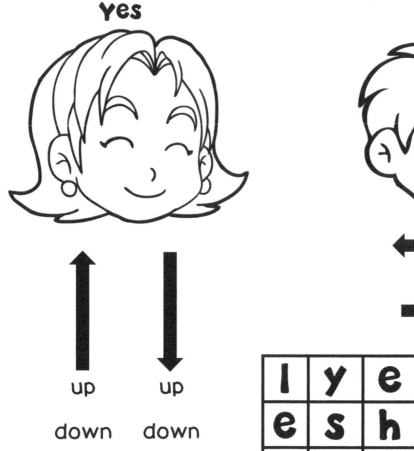

yes

No

up   up

side

down   down

side

Trace the words.

nod

shake

l	y	e	s	r	n
e	s	h	h	f	o
m	m	a	a	b	d
n	o	n	K	g	b
u	s	K	e	w	e

Find the words in the word search.

yes   nod

no   shake

Behavior Skills Printables

Name:_____

What is a Tantrum?

Definition:

An outburst of crying, yelling, falling to the floor or other behaviors done at the same time.

tantrum

DIRECTIONS: Color in the word that that means a person has an outburst of crying, yelling and other behaviors at the same time.

tantrum   self-control

Circle, then write the word you want to use more often:

self-control _or_ tantrum

_____

- -

_____

Name:_____

Why is He Doing This?

Tommy has fallen to the floor and started to cry and move his hands and legs. His teacher is confused and she does not know why.

Why do you think he might be doing this?

He wants a toy.

It is too loud.

His skin hurts.

He doesn't want to go.

What are <u>2</u> ways that he can tell that he wants something?

words   pictures   tears

Draw a line to match the letter on the top to the letter on the bottom.

Name:_____

Giving Up a Turn on Technology

Cut and paste the numbers in descending order to show the kids when their technology time will be over.

Technology Count Down Board

4

1

3

2

Turn
is
over.

This page is intentionally blank due to an activity on the next page.

Name:_____

Drinking Your Own Drink

These girls have trouble remembering which drink they can have and which drink they can't have. Color the pictures of the drinks the girls can drink. Leave blank

Her own drink.

Her own juice box.

Her teacher's drink.

A water fountain drink.

What Can I do With My Hands?

Color the 4 pictures that show what you should do with your hands.

Trace the words that show what you can do with your hands.

high five

handshake

point

wave

Name:_____

It's Too Loud in Here

Trace the words.

| too loud | quiet | shhh |

Mark the words loud & quiet.

loud   play

run   loud

quiet   more

game   quiet

It's too loud.

Tim is in class and the noise volume is too loud, what 3 things can he say?

(too loud)

(be quiet)

(Keep doing this)

(shhh)

This page is intentionally blank due to an activity on the next page.

Name:_____

Not all of the Time

Directions: Cut on the dashed lines. Match the picture to the correct sentence.

Jules loves her crayon box.

She wants to look at it all of the time but in school she has to focus on her work.

She knows that she can look at the crayon box after her work is done.

She decided that she can practice self-control by working first, then looking at her crayon box later.

This page is intentionally blank due to an activity on the next page.

Behavior Skills Printables

Name:_____

Exercise to De-Stress

cross arms

jump

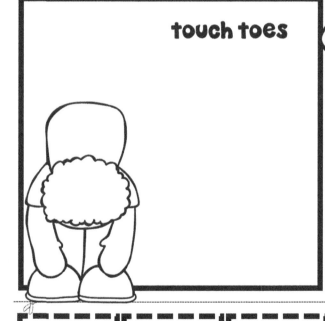

touch toes

arms up

This page is intentionally blank due to an activity on the next page.

Name:_____

What Helps Me Calm Down?

Directions: Color in the pictures of activities that help you feel calm.

squeezing

jumping jacks

beanbag

walking

pushing a wall

CALMING Strategies

music

This page is intentionally blank due to an activity on the next page.

Name:_____

Behavior Words

Match the picture to the word.

kind

gentle

friendly

self-control

gentle 	kind 
friendly 	self-control

This page is intentionally blank due to an activity on the next page.

Name:_____

Keeping Property Safe

Directions: Color the picture that shows the proper way to keep property safe.

read books

or

cut books

drink your drink

or

throw your
drink

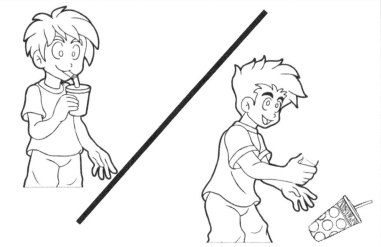

listen to the
lesson

or

push furniture

Keeping Property Safe 2

Directions: Look at each picture. Point to "yes" if the picture shows the correct way to interact with materials. Point to "no" if it shows an incorrect way to interact with materials. Color in the pictures showing the correct actions.

YES   NO

autismCLASSROOM.com

THANK YOU FOR YOUR PURCHASE.

AutismClassroom.com offers books and resources for Special Education and General Education. We make materials to bring out the best in your students with autism and similar needs.

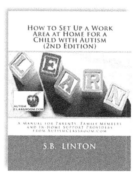

Website: www.autismclassroom.com
Teachers Pay Teachers: www.TeachersPayTeachers.com/Store/Autism-Classroom
Instagram: www.Instagram.com/autismclassroom
Facebook: www.Facebook.com/Autism-Classroom-30958373294

SPECIAL THANKS.

Some of the clip art and fonts were created by the following artists.

Educlips
Rossey's Jungle
Jessica Stanford Fonts
KB3 Teach

autismCLASSROOM.com

CHECK ONLINE FOR MORE PRINTABLES FROM AUTISMCLASSROOM.COM

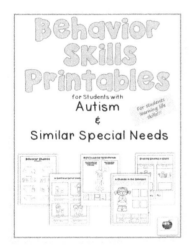

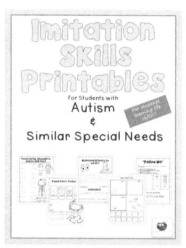

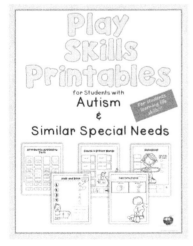

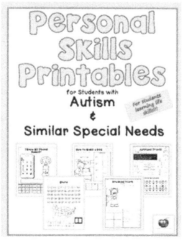

97008398R00079